CW00363061

First published by Bloomsbury Books
an imprint of The Godfrey Cave Group
42 Bloomsbury Street
London WC1B 3QJ

© The Godfrey Cave Group, 1995
© Savitri Books Ltd (all illustrations), 1995

ISBN 1-85471-657-3

All rights reserved. No part of this publication may be
reproduced, stored in a retrieval system, or transmitted
in any form or by any means, electronic, mechanical,
photocopying, recording or otherwise, without
the prior permission of the copyright owners.

Conceived and designed by Savitri Books Ltd
Printed and bound in Great Britain

The illustrations in this book are the work of
Agnieszka Sikorska who is a Polish artist living in Gdansk.
She specialises in restoration work and also teaches
at the School of Art in Gdansk.
She and her husband run an art gallery.
They have two children and
Agnieszka's other passion is cats.

MISCHIEVOUS CATS
DAYBOOK

Illustrated by
Agnieszka Sikorska

Bloomsbury
Books

JANUARY
1999 .

1

2

3

January

4

5

6

7

8

9

10

January   11

12

13

14

15

16

17

January   18

19

20

21

22

23

24

January

25

26

Mothers Birthday. 27

28

29

30

31

FEBRUARY

1

2

3

February

4

5

6

7

8

9

10

February   11

12

13

14

15

16

17

February

18

19

20

21

22

23

24

February 25

26

27

L: George, Stamford. Lunch 28/29

Notes

MARCH

Mon.   1

David Higham's 21st.   2

3

March

4

5

6

7

James Birthday.   8

9

10

March

11

12

13

14

15

16

17

March

18

19

20

21

22

23

24

March

25

26

27

28

29

30

31

APRIL

....

1

....

2

....

3

April 4

5

6

7

8

9

10

April 11

....

12

....

13

....

14

....

15

....

16

....

17

April

18

19

20

21

22

23

24

April

25

26

27

28

29

30

Notes

MAY

1

2

3

May

4

5

6

7

8

9

10

May 11

....

12

....

13

....

14

....

15

....

16

....

17

May

18

19

20

21

22

23

24

May

25

26

27

28

29

30

31

JUNE

1

2

3

June   4

....

5

....

6

....

7

....

8

....

9

....

10

June

11

12

13

14

15

16

17

June

18

19

20

21

22

23

24

June   25

....
                            26

....
                            27

....
                            28

....
                            29

....
                            30

....
                          Notes

JULY

1

2

3

July   4

....
                        5

....
                        6

....
                        7

....
                        8

....
                        9

....
                        10

July

11

12

13

14

15

16

17

July   18

....
                               19

....
                               20

....
                               21

....
                               22

....
                               23

....
                               24

July

25

26

27

28

29

30

31

AUGUST

....
1

....
2

....
3

August

4

5

6

7

8

9

10

August   11

....
                          12

....
                          13

....
                          14

....
                          15

....
                          16

....
                          17

August   18

19

20

21

22

23

24

August 25

26

27

28

29

30

31

SEPTEMBER

1

2

3

September

4

5

6

7

8

9

10

September

11

12

13

14

15

16

17

September   **18**

....

19

....

20

....

21

....

22

....

23

....

24

September   **25**

26

27

28

29

30

Notes

OCTOBER

....

1

....

2

....

3

October

4

5

6

7

8

9

10

October 11

12

13

14

15

16

17

October

18

19

20

21

22

23

24

October

25

26

27

28

29

30

31

NOVEMBER

....
1

....
2

....
3

November

4

5

6

7

8

9

10

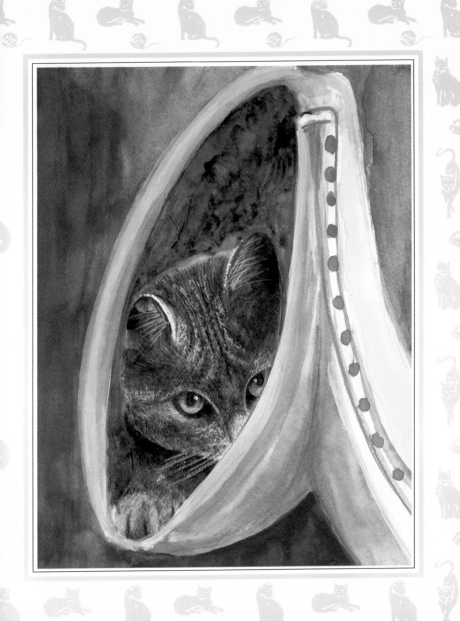

November

11

12

13

14

15

16

17

November

18

19

20

21

22

23

24

November   **25**

....

26

....

27

....

28

....

29

....

30

....

Notes

DECEMBER

....

1

....

2

....

3

December

4

5

6

7

8

9

10

December 11

12

13

14

15

16

17

December

18

19

20

21

22

23

24

December	25

26

27

28

29

30

31